WHEN BEING ME NO LONGER HURTS.......
SURVIVED & CONQUERED

BY
MARIAN D. JONES

When Being Me No Longer Hurts: Survived & Conquered

Copyright © 2020 Marian D. Jones

All rights reserved. This book or any portion thereof may not be reproduced or used in any manner whatsoever without the express written permission of the author except for the use of brief quotations in a book review. Printed in the United States of America Book

First Printing

ISBN 978-1-943284-74-0 pbk

ISBN 978-1-943284-82-5 ebk

A2Z Books Publishing Lithonia, GA 30058 www.A2ZBooksPublishing.net Manufactured in the United States of America A2Z Books Publishing has allowed this work to remain exactly as the publisher intended.

Revelation 21:4

He will wipe every tear from their eyes There will be no more death or mourning or crying or pain for the old order of things has passed away

Contents

Divorce Part I 1
Divorce Part II 3
Abuse Part I 6
Abuse Part II 8
Parenting Part I 11
Parenting Part II 13
Incarceration Part I 17
Incarceration Part II 19
Incarceration Part III 21
Incarceration Part IV 23
Incarceration Part V 25
Incarceration Part VI 27
Love Part I 30
Love Part II 32
Love Part III 34
Family Part I 38
Family Part II 40
Cancer Part I 44
Cancer Part II 46
Cancer Part III 48
Cancer Part IV 50
Cancer Part V 52
Summary 56

Divorce Part I

He heals the brokenhearted and binds up their wounds. (Psalm 147:3)

Saying I do with the person that carried your heart close and promised you a lifetime of love, sure not always good times, but they felt good because you were able to share them with someone that loved you and made a vow to honor and respect you for better or worse.

One day the better turns worse, the tiny drops of rain felt like a never-ending thunderstorm, days turned into months of pain, disrespect, and Hate! Who knew the end of your job would cause so much distant with the one that promised to love you no matter the situation, but what about me loving you through the words that tore me into shreds of low self-esteem, loving you through the empty nights of you not returning home, loving you through the many times of "I'm sorry it will never happen again."

Now the bills are coming seems like daily and not monthly and the money is just not enough, so coming home is truly not an option for you any longer, because what really am, I coming home to …. Your eyes look pass me with so much pain that it pierces the very inner of my soul respect turns into disrespect; purpose turns into pain, and the love that once drew us close has torn us completely apart and now

MARIAN D. JONES

decisions that we both hate to make or at least me….Have to be made

Every day another rejection, trying to hold on to my third marriage and not fill like a failure once again. Why is it so

Divorce Part II

❖

He heals the brokenhearted and binds up their wounds. (Psalm 147:3)

Is it hard for you to love me when the times get hard, are is it just hard to love me…? And what is the definition of love? And who determines that it's correct!

However, that once again is a dream and not our reality. Making it work is something you refuse to talk about or consider. You would think that I would have this marriage thing down, and fixing us was one of the hardest things to do, especially when the person you love no longer loves you are cares that the marriage is ending.

Every day I give and take much more than I should because I need/want it to work. So, when you decide not to come home or call, I roll over and look at the clock until once again the sun comes up and another day to maybe hear you say, "Let's try to make it work," "marriage can endure pain and have a purpose."

Notes

NOTES

Abuse Part I

Husbands love your wives and do not be harsh with them. Colossians 3:19

So, this is what love really feels like… you must really love me because this hurts like hell! But a little more make-up over that eye, and no one will even notice that it's puffy and purple. Wait, how about I wear the designer sunglasses tonight to work, and everyone will just think I'm cool….

Growing up my father taught me everything about Abuse, he wore the crown for being the king of abuse to my mother and me and my sisters; however, I just didn't get enough of the slaps across my mom's face, the rape, the gun that should have killed her or the mere disrespect in front of friends and family, just not enough, so I married an abuser…..

Yes, that's love my mama stayed, so I got this, nothing to do just do what he says, and no matter what, it's always your fault, and it will never happen again, and things will work out just fine. Until that one day, he raises his hand to slap your daughter, and you get brave and push him down………. now his hands are around my neck, and you're gasping for air until he falls down, and you inhale so deeply that you think it's your very last breathe!

WHEN BEING ME NO LONGER HURTS.......

Another day and yet another slap in the face, another harsh word, and more sunglasses and make-up that hides the scars but not the guilt and shame. Just maybe if I make his favorite meal or wear that dress that he likes to see me in the pain want be as bad the next time….. Sleeping with the enemy takes on a new meaning when it becomes your reality….easing your way out of bed thinking just maybe you can leave and you

MARIAN D. JONES

Abuse Part II

Husbands love your wives and do not be harsh with them. Colossians 3:19

Make it out the door only to return home, and yes, he's gone, but there's a note on the bed that says, "I'll be back and you better me here" too afraid to leave or tell anyone your truth!

When is enough, ENOUGH! IS IT EVER ENOUGH! IS IT REALLY MY FAULT! HE SAID SORRY! YESTERDAY WAS A GOOD Day. He came home last night. My family loves him and thinks he treats me nicely. My kids never want for anything; all the bills are paid and on time.

Does stability erase the pain of abuse, or do we just look at it differently because of fear of starting over alone………

Notes

Notes

Parenting Part I

Whoever spares the rod hates their children, but the one who loves their children is careful to discipline them. (Proverbs 13:24)

Parenting where is the book of how to effectively raise kids, especially for those times when they know it all, hate you, but mom, my friends, are going!

Learning to parent when no one taught you how….growing up seems like a part of my memories that I've erased. Maybe the pain of seeing my father treat my mother with such disrespect and abuse allowed be to cover/ suppress all the times that just maybe we really did have a good time, just maybe we went out as a family without any confusion or fights! Just maybe….

Having daughters that call me mom allow me to want and do things differently, did I always get it right? No, of course not, but I did my best with what I knew. Parenting from a hurt place and a dark place is hard because you try so hard to find your way and not totally lose it in the end.

Remembering the times when my daughter leaves my home and said she hated me and that I never cared for her was a hurt place, but I'm still a mom! Knowing that even when she says you never sent me a birthday card, never stood with me when at least I thought that you should, and always taking my sister's side.

Never understanding that while in my thinking it was protecting them, it was causing more pain to myself because I wanted to be there wanted to provide more financially, but I still needed healing in order to parent them in a good place. Even knowing the right things to say to others concerning

Parenting Part II

Whoever spares the rod hates their children, but the one who loves their children is careful to discipline them. (Proverbs 13:24)

Their children, but what about saying and doing the right things concerning my own family.

Parenting comes with no rules, regulations, policies, guidelines, dos, and don'ts. But instead, trial and error and often one outweighs the other, and the process of both hurts like hell! But we never give up because we birthed this child, and although we may not have done it right today, God's grace and mercy allow us another chance to get it right.

Getting it right…what's right? Giving sound advice that will allow them to make good godly decisions so when they are parents, they're able to look back and remember that you taught them to love each other no matter what the situation, help each other however not to hinder. Allow them to find their way but never stop encouraging, praying, and speaking life even when the situation looks dead!

When do we get it, right? Does it ever seem or get right? Maybe not; however, don't quit!! That child/situation that you think will never change, that pain that you feel will never heal, it will get better, it will heal.

……….they will once again love and respect the times you said the hard words that really did hurt you more than it did them. So yes, parenting hurts, but it also heals.

Notes

Notes

Incarceration Part I

--- ❖ ---

Even though I walk through the darkest valley, I will fear no evil, for you are with me; your rod and your staff, they comfort me. (Psalm 23:4)

Incarceration! I remember this day as if it happened this morning…… my life of writing bad checks to various merchants and being in and out of jail and God allowed me to be overcome with his loving grace and mercy each time I presented a check that I knew was bad. However, in my mind, I needed that dress, those shoes, that cell phone for my daughters because why not every child at school had one and I wanted to give them everything I wasn't given as a child, no matter the cost of the penalty.

The night before the court, I took the time to talk with my daughter making them aware that I would be standing before a judge in the morning, and it was in God's hands to what would happen. Didn't know if I would return home after court or not. But I loved them no matter what the outcome.

November 4, 2008, I stood before Judge Langston with a stolen money order in my hand to pay off my fines. I had missed several appointments with my probation officer, and yet I just wanted to make the payments and return to work and my life as usual, not this day!

The judge heard the plea from my attorney, and without blinking an eye, his gavel hit the desk! 3 years in the Arkansas department of correction……the breath left my body, and I imagined that this was a dream, no I have money in my hand! No, I

Incarceration Part II

❖

Even though I walk through the darkest valley, I will fear no evil, for you are with me; your rod and your staff, they comfort me. (Psalm 23:4)

Have a job, children, responsibilities, I want to do it again, I've learned my lesson!

All of this sounded great; however, it was too late. Have a seat the officer said and wait there until we can escort you back to the Pulaski county jail, awaiting your departure to the Arkansas department of correction to serve out your sentence.

I immediately thought about my children and all that I would miss in the three years of not seeing them for birthdays, holidays, and those memories that I would never get back. Breanna would have her 16th birthday without me to help her celebrate! Casse would play an entire season of basketball, not able to look in the stands and see her number one fan cheering her on as she made the winning shot that would make the team eligible to play in the championship!

So, I wait with thoughts of depression running through my head, how did this happen? It was not supposed to happen this way! God, you abandoned me when I needed you the most!!! I trusted you, and I prayed to go home, not to jail!

Now the short ride to arrive at the jail seems like hours, and we arrive, and the process begins. Mugshots, fingerprinting, paperwork, orange jumpsuits, mattress, one sheet, one blanket, shower shoes……………
this is my life for what I image

Incarceration Part III

Even though I walk through the darkest valley, I will fear no evil, for you are with me; your rod and your staff, they comfort me. (Psalm 23:4)

As three long years, however, to my dismay, you're given two months on a year in state time, so that means I will only have to serve 7 months……. good news not really……..time is just time long or short. Missing everything because everything changes and for the next time away from family and life as I've known it for 44 years with now become a memory until I return home.

Now spending each night in a small cold room with concrete walls, thin mattress and one blanket that never allows you to get warm but just covers up to half your body….my life living with a stranger that committed murder to a man that raped her daughter, her reliving this incident and getting mad at everyone outside of this little room when they say she was wrong and then back in this small room with all that anger still present in her mind and heart….sleeping with the enemy……stranger in my room……..danger close by………

The first night seems like hell! You think it's a dream and will wake up like on so many other days in jail and go to court receive a bond, and my mom gets me out, and I go home and go back to work and start my life over…….not this time more wake-ups in this place that has now become home. Eat early and no matter when you're hungry again there's not a kitchen

Incarceration Part IV

❖

Even though I walk through the darkest valley, I will fear no evil, for you are with me; your rod and your staff, they comfort me. (Psalm 23:4)

At your disposal to get more food; however, the first plate was awful, so you eat the bread and drink the water just to stay healthy enough, so your head no longer hurts, and your blood pressure stays under control.

Receiving medical attention in the county jail is a process (not a short process), but it finally happens, and you receive medication as required. One month down and another roommate Federal drug charges, boy did she really have some stories, in and out of jail since she was very young now much older than me and many others that were housed in this jail unit with us. She knew the guards by name, and they knew her because she was a regular (not my testimony) she smuggled drugs on her body in a plane to Mexico made it cross the border and got caught on the way back spent years in a Mexican jail and returned back to the states to face federal charges once again because like I said she was a regular.

Many long nights and more roommates, nasty food. But now I have money on my books, and I can buy snacks and get a phone card to call home…my first call to my mother, can't breathe pass the tears and shame of her knowing everything that I constantly lied about to everyone. Yes, I went to see my parole officer, yes, I paid my fees, no, I don't have court.

Incarceration Part V

Even though I walk through the darkest valley, I will fear no evil, for you are with me; your rod and your staff, they comfort me. (Psalm 23:4)

But her voice was calm and forgiving even before I asked for forgiveness. Her assuring me that my daughters would like me fine living with her until my return. So now continuing to live my

Life behind bars away from family, friends, and a life that I love.

More phone calls, visits, letters, and tears………. but one day, the letters went from blaming others to taking total accountability for everything that caused me to be behind bars. The lies, the bad checks, the stealing, the trust in myself, and not totally relying on God and those that really wanted to help me heal!

I remember talking to my mom and asking about the girls, and she told me that Breanna, my oldest daughter, attempted to kill herself by taking some pills! This broke my heart for I immediately blamed myself for not being in a place where I was able to protect her, my mom reassured me that she was good, and I later was able to talk with her and not blame myself for what I was unable to change.

So now, I've allowed the time to heal me and not make me bitter and angry at God for my mistakes. I wrote letters to everyone that I hurt. Sisters, daughters, mother, and friends. The hardest letter to write was to my deceased father releasing

Incarceration Part VI

--- ❖ ---

Even though I walk through the darkest valley, I will fear no evil, for you are with me; your rod and your staff, they comfort me. (Psalm 23:4)

All the hurt and pain that he caused me that allowed me not to love completely (this healing was painful however thank you, Pastor Jagers, for letting me know it was necessary)

Letters and cards kept me encouraged; there was never a day that a card was not received from my dear friend/sister Janet; she lived in Kansas City and was unable to visit, but whenever anyone in her family came to Arkansas, they came to see me on her behave. krissye came every week, and we laughed, talked, and prayed.

Seeing my mom through that glass broke my heart, and when I returned to my room, I cried, for I know that her heart broke to know the mistakes I made, which caused her pain. I read some hard letters from my sisters that really made me see the pain and shame caused by my actions………there was purpose through that pain, and it hurt like hell! But it healed the very core of my pain and allowed me to see who God purposed me to become no matter the process or the road not easily traveled, and it truly birthed me into better.

Notes

Notes

MARIAN D. JONES

Love Part I

❖

Love is patient, and love is kind. It does not envy, and it does not boast, it is not proud. It does not dishonor others, it is not self-seeking, it is not easily angered, and it keeps no record of wrongs. Love does not delight in evil but rejoices with the truth. It always protects, always trusts hopes, and always perseveres.

Love never fails. But where there are prophecies, they will cease; where there are tongues, they will be stilled; where there is knowledge, it will pass away. (I Corinthians 13:4-8)

What's the meaning of real love, does pain come with that are just happiness and joy no matter the circumstance or situation, you take a licking and keep on ticking, right! You take love to the next level marriage, and you remember your vows, but when the worse outweigh, the better you wonder if it's really worth it, yes sometimes you worse is really worse but no matter what the love is an eternal commitment. So you press your way even throughout the worse!

Love is defined as an intense feeling of deep affection, wow what an awesome example of love, love is so remarkable and different in many ways. We love our children no matter what they allow us to endure we love our parents no matter the choices and decisions they have to make concerning our life, we love our siblings even when we no longer agree have no same goals in mind.

Love is hanging on to something that has allowed you to lose yourself, but God says now is not the time to let go, so you wait until it doesn't hurt as much, and you continue to hang on. Love

Love Part II

Love is patient, and love is kind. It does not envy, and it does not boast, it is not proud. It does not dishonor others, it is not self-seeking, it is not easily angered, and it keeps no record of wrongs. Love does not delight in evil but rejoices with the truth. It always protects, always trusts hopes, and always perseveres.

Love never fails. But where there are prophecies, they will cease; where there are tongues, they will be stilled; where there is knowledge, it will pass away. (I Corinthians 13:4-8)

Is knowing the truth but not saying it because it will not only hurt you but those that you love.

I never knew what true love felt like until I had my daughters and although they have sometimes brought tears to my eyes they are certainly one of God's greatest gifts to me and have had an impact on my life even the bad days with them are good days, and that's because of the everlasting love that has impacted my heart for life!

Love when it hurts! Love when it ignores! Love when it dies! Love!!! Learning to embrace your battle scars and turn them into beauty marks.

Love is patient: take the time to love yourself and allow others to embrace the love that you can give instead of taking the love out of you for granted.

Love is kind: it doesn't hurt on purpose; it takes the time to be nice no matter how you feel or how the situation. Love is calm!

Love does not envy: never resent my past and the love I have for others and compare it to the love I have for you!

MARIAN D. JONES

Love Part III

❖

Love is patient, and love is kind. It does not envy, and it does not boast, it is not proud. It does not dishonor others, it is not self-seeking, it is not easily angered, and it keeps no record of wrongs. Love does not delight in evil but rejoices with the truth. It always protects, always trusts hopes, and always perseveres.

Love never fails. But where there are prophecies, they will cease; where there are tongues, they will be stilled; where there is knowledge, it will pass away. (I Corinthians 13:4-8)

Love does not boast and is not proud: don't take the time to boast and be proud regarding all the things they've accomplished.

Love does not dishonor others/ self-seeking: don't take the time to dishonor the pain that has been caused by another person.

Love is not easily angered: everything is doesn't require an argument or disagreement, take the time to talk it out.

WHEN BEING ME NO LONGER HURTS.......

LOVE KEEPS NO RECORD OF WRONGS: WHEN YOU SAY YOU'RE SORRY AND FORGIVE IS GIVEN DON'T BRING IT BACK UP TO HUIRT AGAIN!

LOVE DOES NOT DELIGHT IN EVIL BUT REJOICES WITH THE TRUTH: WRONG IS NOT A HAPPY PLACE; however, THE TRUTH ALLOWS YOU TO BE GLAD!

LOVE ALWAYS PROTECTS, TRUSTS, HOPES, AND PRE-SERVES: PROTECTION- CARING FOR ME AND MAKING SURE EVERYTHING AND EVERYONE IN OUR FAMILY IS SAFE!

TRUSTS- NEVER DOUBTING THE WORDS NO MATTER THE GOSSIP HOPES- LOVING THE PRESERVES-

Notes

Notes

MARIAN D. JONES

Family Part I

❖

So in everything, do to others what you would have them do to you, for this sums up the Law and the Prophets. (matthew7:12)

Family; a group consisting of parents and children living together in a household; family all the descendants of a common ancestor.

The family you all born to the same mother and father in my case, we endured the same upbringing, same love, same discipline, same laughter, same pain, same memories.

Sisters that love you, sisters that tolerate you, sisters that love when it's comfortable, sisters that love in the face of others, sisters that love, so no one talks about the real problems because we are the sisters that in everyone sight that has always got along and never argued because we are sisters that love!

When did it all change? Why did it all change? What brought us to this change? What changed? Still, no answers to these questions, even when I asked no one has the correct answer, however, it just continues to lead to more questions that allow for me to feel guilty for an empty space that I didn't create.

I remember when things were normal, and they included me in all the conversations regarding life, everyday things how the family was doing how things had changed within the family, but now it's hard to even have a normal conversation without addressing the elephant in the room that no one seems to address, are we just choose not to talk about it at all.

However, in reality, it really has just turned into I'll only communicate when it's necessary, absolutely necessary

MARIAN D. JONES

Family Part II

2 So in everything, do to others what you would have them do to you, for this sums up the Law and the Prophets. (Matthew 7:12)

And so again I rise! Rise above what you think of me! Rise above what you say about me! Rise above my past! And rise to my future!

Do you ever not hold me hostage from my past! I did the crime; however, the crime did not make me bitter but better! Family, what does it really mean; born in the same house and grow up loving each other, but what happens when you finally really grow up and have your own voice, and it speaks louder than anything that will come out of their mouths!

Even your silence speaks volumes! Realizing that I had to endure everything that hurt to conquer and embrace my healing, so thank you family for every word that pushed me to my healing, thank you family for every time you spoke negatively regarding the decisions that made me get a bolder voice and speak out loud!

Thank you, family, for allowing me to see the real me and realizing that often my silence was the pain. The months of no calls allowed me to face me to say I apologize no matter what I did or didn't do. Thank you, family for loving me throughout the pain that sometimes you caused, and I never addressed it and just kept going because I just wanted everyone to once again to be happy no matter if I had to pay the ultimate price for the happiness.

So today, my love is better, stronger, and my voice is heard through my life and not my tears and silence!

Notes

Notes

MARIAN D. JONES

Cancer Part I

❖

But he was pierced for our transgressions; he was crushed for our iniquities; the punishment that brought us peace was on him, and by his wounds, we are healed. Isaiah 53:5

Regular wellness exam determines you need to schedule your yearly mammogram, no problem, so before you leave the office, they have you scheduled. The day comes for mammogram appointment, and you attend and leave there and go to work, days pass, and a call comes that you need a second mammogram for a better look.

That day comes and goes, and yet another call that brings you to worry but not much because Breast Cancer is nowhere in my family, so now a Biopsy is scheduled. Appointment day and my blood pressure are very high, and the physician determines that she wants to reschedule until it's better, so now I wait another week and wonder just what will happen if the results are positive.

Well, second appointment, biopsy complete results in 2-3 days, so I go home and return to work on the next day. The days seem like weeks and months, and then the call comes while at work.

Mrs. Jones, this is Ouachita Medical Center with your Biopsy results it has been determined that you have Invasive Ductal Carcinoma (Breast Cancer) in my right breast, someone from Dr. Abraham office will call you to schedule an appointment to go over results and next steps with you and your family…………..

Wow what do I do now……..Call my husband, and he reassures that part of my heart that has skipped a beat and says no matter what God is in control, I smile through the tears and can feel his arms embracing that part of me that is afraid. Next call my Mom, got my results and its Breast Cancer……No, are you alright? Yes, mam, I know that God is a Healer, and this process is necessary for the purpose of my journey. I really wanted just to break down and fall on the floor and just cry; however, my faith in God would not allow the natural part of my life to crumble in front of me.

So I grab my keys and take a drive a few blocks from my office to Cassandra Vaughn she comes outside of her office, and I BREAK! Through the tears, I give her the news, and she covers me in prayer and lets me know that she will be a

Cancer Part II

But he was pierced for our transgressions; he was crushed for our iniquities; the punishment that brought us peace was on him, and by his wounds, we are healed.
Isaiah 53:5

Constant support throughout this Journey and will also reach out to others that will cover me in prayer.

So I return to work and finish my entire day, the call from Dr. Abraham office came. She schedules an appointment with my family and me to go over every detail and for me to make necessary changes for my Journey of Healing.

This was on Friday, June 28th we asked all the hard questions and got answers that reassured us that with the Grace of God all things would work out in his time, the process would be mine, and however, God ordained it to be for my life in this season. So after a careful conversation with God and my husband, we decided on Monday, July 8th, to have a Double mastectomy/Reconstruction Surgery, which was scheduled for August 6th. This process was long and produced a lot of pain one overnight stay in the hospital then home for the road to recovery. Weekly trips to Little Rock for Plastic Surgeon visits to make sure my drains are not infected until they can be out and then proceed with the expansion of tissue expanders.

So last day of tissue expanders was on September 4 now Chemo I will begin (8) rounds that will start every other Thursday on September 12, first round was HELL!!! I was nausea, tried, dehydrated, infection in body, fever ……But God! I made it to my mom's house for the weekend just to lay in her bed and visit with her, I was sick the entire weekend, but I was with my mama!

So the weekend was over, and my husband came to get me and the night was still bad, and so the next morning I had to go to the hospital and had IV fluids and antibiotic IV with blood so I go home and I feel better and the second round of Chemo my blood counts are still very low, so my oncologist who is AMAZING Dr. Lynn Cleveland takes the time to adjust my medication and makes this cycle better for my body and just one round of nausea and vomiting

MARIAN D. JONES

Cancer Part III

❖

**But he was pierced for our transgressions, and he was crushed for our iniquities; the punishment that brought us peace was on him, and by his wounds, we are healed.
Isaiah 53:5**

And constipation, so I'm learning what makes me feel good and how your taste buds will not be the same, and what you once ate so much of really doesn't taste the same anymore.

Learning to adjust my sleeping habits to take pills because I really do need them and remember to rest and eat and take time for me and enjoy the journey.

I know that God has purposed this journey for such a time as this in my life, I love every journey of my life the Heartache, the Tears, The Pain that hurt so much in my life that I really never knew if I would ever overcome Divorce, Abuse, Incarceration, Hate.

The third round of Chemo went very well nausea but no vomit, was able to work and finish a big deadline with no delays, and so even in the midst of what the enemy would want me to believe would be the worst part of my life has saved me on so many levels.

This season/journey of my life has taught me about me and how life changes in a blinking of an eye and it's so important to listen to the still voice of God and make sure you're true to the real you no matter what others may say God really does Love the very worst part of me I am truly a testament that God can turn a mess into ministry!

This season of Faith, Love, Peace, Joy, and anointing is the best JOURNEY God has ever blessed me to endure. I've watched my children grow into wonderful, amazing Adults! And God has blessed me with Amazing Loving Friends and Family that have walked me through some painful nights and days. I have a Mother that has a Heart of Gold that has allowed me just to be me even in my weakest moments; she just let me be me, and she didn't allow me to stay there but brought me right back to me!

Janet, what could I say about you, you inspired me in every way throughout the miles, tears, letters, gifts, and the cutting of my Hair!

Cancer Part IV

**But he was pierced for our transgressions; he was crushed for our iniquities; the punishment that brought us peace was on him, and by his wounds, we are healed.
Isaiah 53:5**

My NHC Church Family exactly what church really is not just talking about God and what he means in your life and how they will not leave any stone unturned to make sure this journey of healing is not faced alone and they have proved that over and over (food, cards, text, phone call, fruit, baskets, monetary gifts, balloons, prayers.

The journey gets closer to the end, I now have only one more Chemo Treatment, unable to sleep in my bed because it's uncomfortable, and my skin is dark in areas that was once light. As I near this end, I wanted to celebrate my coming out with a photoshoot with all the people that meant a lot to me and helped encourage me along this journey.

Although this meant so much to me, others seem to not see it as important, so although the level of importance wasn't great, it meant the world to my Children and Husband, and they will take the time to allow it to happen!

WHEN BEING ME NO LONGER HURTS.......

There is never a part of my life that I intend to allow someone to disregard. I've developed into a strong God-fearing woman that has faced many challenging and came out a winner!! So I will no longer be hostage to what others may think of me or the decisions I should have made at the expense of someone else happiness.

I am a survivor of Love, A survivor of Abuse, A survivor of Past Hurts, A survivor of Family Hurt, A Survivor of Incarceration, and A Survivor of CANCER!!!!!

So, Lord, I Thank you for each affliction, I Thank you for each time I got up, and the pain was awful, but I took steps to keep going no matter what the enemy would want me to believe I still Trust God for my Healing I still Trust God for my Deliverance and my Testimony!

Survivor- A person who copes well with difficulties in their life..... Marian Denise Jones…………..

MARIAN D. JONES

Cancer Part V

❖

But he was pierced for our transgressions; he was crushed for our iniquities; the punishment that brought us peace was on him, and by his wounds, we are healed. Isaiah 53:5

Today's the day last round of Chemo!!! WoW where did the time go seems like I just received the news that I had Cancer…and know I've reached the end of this Stage of Healing. Bi-weekly appointments with my oncologist and now finally my 3 month check-up that will determine if I receive a get out of Cancer Free Card! So the entire office embraces me as I arrive and tell me how amazing I look, and they've had really missed seeing my face. They we're super awesome throughout the entire process, so now it's time for my vitals prior to visiting with my oncologist. So now Dr. Cleveland comes in the room, and she first hugs me (as she as always done) she begins to commend me on how well I look and how proud she is of me taking Chemo so easy. My blood work shows NO CANCER, so she ends the visit with CANCER FREE see you in 3 months!!(Insert a shout around the entire room), so now the final chapter happens ………Breast Reconstruction surgery with Dr. David Bauer.

Surgery has been scheduled for Monday, March 16th @12:00 noon. Although we have entered into unfamiliar territory with the Coronavirus-19, my surgery is as planned. Certain precautions are taken, leading to this day so that my immune system is not compromised. Surgery was a success, and with minimum pain afterward, no overnight stay in the hospital long ride home pain meds and bed. However, drains were inserted after surgery, but only two (2) this time, if there is less than 20cc on Thursday, they can both be removed. Thursday comes, and I made it with less than 10cc, so I cut the suture line and remove the drains.

So now waiting for the good report from my follow-up appointment on Monday. This has really been an emotional journey for me at times, not really knowing if been positive and trusting God was going to be enough, even when the good reports came in I still wanted to doubt God had healed my body.

Notes

Notes

MARIAN D. JONES

Summary

❖

Love is patient, and love is kind. It does not envy, and it does not boast, it is not proud. It does not dishonor others, it is not self-seeking, it is not easily angered, and it keeps no record of wrongs. Love does not delight in evil but rejoices with the truth. It always protects, always trusts hopes, and always perseveres.

Love never fails. But where there are prophecies, they will cease; where there are tongues, they will be stilled; where there is knowledge, it will pass away. (I Corinthians 13:4-8)

What's the meaning of real love, does pain come with that are just happiness and joy no matter the circumstance or situation, you take a licking and keep on ticking, right! You take love to the next level marriage, and you remember your vows, but when the worse outweigh, the better you wonder if it's really worth it, yes sometimes your bad ends up being your worst , but no matter what the love is an eternal commitment. So you press your way even throughout the bad!

Love is defined as an intense feeling of deep affection, wow what an awesome example of love, love is so remarkable and different in many ways. We love our children no matter what they allow us to endure, we love our parents no matter the choices, and decisions they have to make concerning our life, we love our siblings even when we no longer agree and have none of the same goals in mind.

Love is hanging on to something that has allowed you to lose yourself, but God says now is not the time to let go, so you wait until it doesn't hurt as much, and you continue to hang on.

Marian Jones writes this book and prays that each page will allow your release from Abuse, Love and Incarceration to free you completely. This book was inspired through life experiences that pushed purpose from my pain and allowed me to silence the chatter in my head and heal!

mrsjcjones01@gmail.com

Interested in Writing and/or Publishing a Book?
Visit www.a2zbookspublishing.net

www.ingramcontent.com/pod-product-compliance
Lightning Source LLC
Chambersburg PA
CBHW052123110526
44592CB00013B/1728